CHINA

© Aladdin Books Ltd 1987

Designed and produced by
Aladdin Books Ltd
70 Old Compton Street
London W1

First published in
Great Britain in 1987 by
Franklin Watts
12a Golden Square
London W1

ISBN 0 86313 595 1

Printed in Belgium

Design — David West Children's Book Design

Editor — Denny Robson

Researcher — Cecilia Weston-Baker

Illustrator — Rob Shone

Consultant — Julia Hutt, Far Eastern Department, Victoria and Albert Museum, London.

The spelling used in this book for Chinese names is the pinyin *romanisation system.*

CONTENTS

INTRODUCTION	4
THE AGE OF CONFLICT 1400-221 BC	6
Confucius: Laozi and Taoism	
Writing: Bronze casting	
Burials: The family	
Ancestor worship	
THE FIRST EMPIRE 221 BC-AD 618	12
Qin Shihuang: The Great Wall	
Life at court: The jade prince	
Medicine: Papermaking	
Science and technology	
THE GOLDEN AGE AD 618-1368	18
Town life	
Theatre: The life of women: Justice	
Buddhism: Trade routes	
Poetry	
IMPERIAL SPLENDOUR AD 1368-1911	25
The emperor and the people: Agriculture	
Porcelain	
Exploration: The Jesuits	
Opium: The Boxer Rebellion	
"LET THE PAST SERVE THE PRESENT"	30
INDEX	32

GREAT CIVILIZATIONS
CHINA
1400 BC–AD 1911

Beth McKillop

FRANKLIN WATTS
London·New York·Toronto·Sydney

INTRODUCTION

China is Asia's largest and most populous country. Its written history dates back over more than 3,000 years, and the Chinese people today are the proud inheritors of a civilization which produced some of the world's finest works of literature and art.

Society in ancient China was divided into aristocrats and common people. Emperors had absolute power over their subjects. Farmers and town dwellers paid taxes of grain and goods to support the government and army. For over 2,000 years, the ideas of Confucius, a philosopher of the sixth century BC, shaped Chinese life. Confucius taught that subjects must obey their rulers and sons must obey their fathers.

The story of China's past starts with myths about the earliest kings. Their heroic and virtuous lives provided an important role-model for later emperors. Until comparatively recently, Chinese government was more concerned to imitate the sages of antiquity than to deal with the world beyond the middle kingdom, as China's name, *Zhong guo* means.

This book describes important scenes in China's past. It is divided into four periods: from the earliest historical times until China was united under one ruler in 221 BC; the first empires; China's golden age, leading into the time of Mongol domination; and the late imperial period, the Ming and Qing dynasties.

Peking man
The most famous forebears of the Chinese nation were a hunting nomadic group who lived over 500,000 years ago – Peking man. Their remains were discovered by archaeologists in 1927. Before then, nothing was known about hunters like the one in our picture, who ate fish and meat and used tools of bone and stone. Peking man was followed by the first farmers, who learned to grow millet and rice and lived in settled communities.

THE AGE OF CONFLICT 1400-221 BC

The earliest historical evidence of Chinese civilization points to the lavish life of the nobility in about 1500 BC. Excavations show that when powerful men died, their servants and belongings were buried with them. Rival kingdoms controlled large parts of the country and wars constantly broke out between them. By the fourth century BC, some smaller states were being defeated and absorbed by their stronger neighbours. Finally in the third century BC, the Qin dynasty imposed control over all China.

A writing system was developed at this time which is clearly related to the way Chinese is written today. Impressive bronze vessels were cast, and iron farm tools were used from the 7th century onwards. Scientific achievements of the time included large-scale irrigation works and astronomical observations.

Weapons, armour and chariot fittings of bronze were used in fierce inter-state battles after Zhou toppled Shang. Known to Chinese historians as the "Warring States" era, this was a time when commoners were conscripted into state armies. Many stories are told of the cunning strategies used by contenders for power against their rivals.

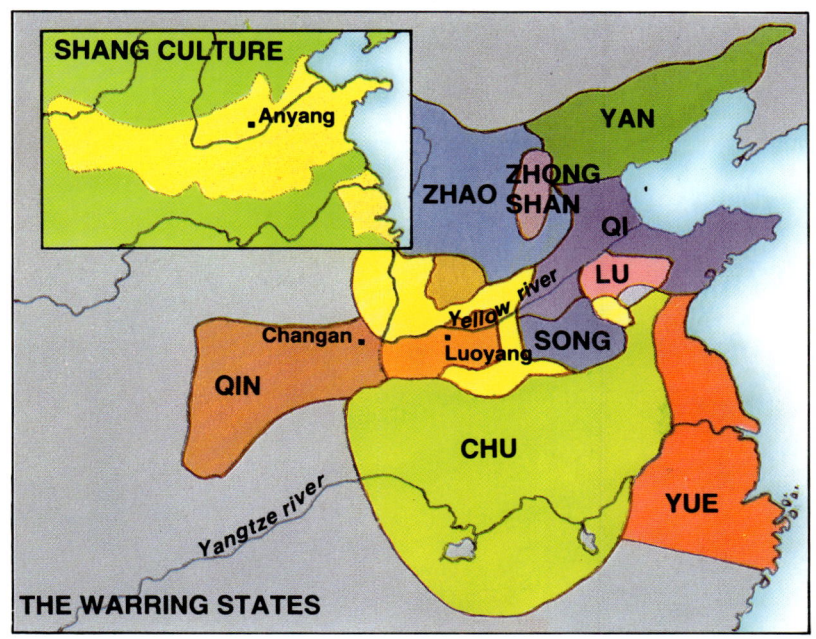

DATECHART

c5000-2000 BC Neolithic period. Agricultural communities with domesticated animals grew up, using decorated baked earthernware pots. No written records survive.

c1500 BC Priests use cracks in heated animal bones to predict the future, writing with symbols related to today's Chinese characters.

c1500-1100 BC The heartland of early Chinese civilization, the Yellow River valley of north-west China, sees the rise of China's first historically recorded rulers, the Shang.

c1400 BC Shang moves its capital to Anyang, a symmetrical city of square buildings where bronze-casting is developed into a highly refined art.

1027 BC King Wu of Zhou overthrows the Shang and founds the Zhou dynasty.

770 BC After invasions by western barbarians, Zhou moves the capital east to Luoyang.

c700 BC Iron is used to make farm tools for the first time.

551 BC Confucius, China's most influential philosopher, is born.

403-221 BC Rival kingdoms fight for control of China, giving rise to the name "Warring States" for this period.

4th and 3rd centuries BC In the west of the country, the state of Qin grows in power and after absorbing Han, Zhao, Wei, Chu and Yan, Qin unifies China in 221 BC.

THE AGE OF CONFLICT

Confucius
Kong Fu zi (Master Kong, or Confucius in Latin) was a travelling philosopher who gave advice to the lords of the warring kingdoms. He taught that kings of past times had ruled by setting a good example to the common people. His book, the *Analects* influenced politicians and scholars for centuries after his death. His disciples included Mencius, who taught that human nature was basically virtuous.

Laozi and Taoism
In contrast to the followers of Confucius, Laozi believed that politics was a futile activity. Laozi taught that the *Tao*, or "Way", reflected the patterns of nature. Taoists (followers of the Way) said that inactivity and contemplation were the only possible course of action for a wise man. Laozi, shown here contemplating nature, wrote a treatise on the Way and thought that people who bustle about trying to improve the world are fools. His philosophy advocated doing nothing ("wu wei") and achieving harmony with nature.

1400-221 BC

Writing

Chinese writing today is closely based on the pictorial characters of Shang times. Beginning by portraying objects (as in the characters for water and field) the writing system built up the ability to convey complicated and abstract ideas. Chinese people have always admired fine calligraphy. The photograph shows a child practising calligraphy in the traditional way.

	Ancestor	Then (Man and bowl)	Prayer	Earth	Field	Water	Pot
Ancient							
Modern	祖	就	祝	土	田	水	鼎

Bronze casting

From Shang times, bronze vessels were cast in a marvellous variety of shapes and guises. No-one knows how the Chinese first learned to make elaborate bronze vessels over 3,000 years ago. But we do know that beautiful, complicated pots, decorated with animal faces and abstract designs, were used for the ceremonies which dominated court life. They were used in sacrifices to the gods, for example. Ordinary people never used bronzes. The picture shows craftsmen preparing molten bronze, ready to mould the hot liquid metal into utensils for ritual use.

9

THE AGE OF CONFLICT

Burials
The early Chinese believed that after death, spirits pass into an afterlife. The spirit had to be in a place with good omens, protected from evil spirits. It was also important for the dead to have their belongings buried alongside them. They needed to be cared for after death in a way which reflected their status in life. Rich people had food and wine vessels and weapons buried with them. This picture shows a nobleman's tomb with horses and servants. A dissatisfied spirit would bring unhappiness to his family. In the case of a king, his subjects would suffer if the tomb was not fine enough.

The family
Confucius' teaching lies at the root of China's traditional family structure. He taught that women had to obey men, and the young must obey the old. Brides always went to live with their husband's family.

1400-221 BC

Ancestor worship
Because the Chinese believe that ancestors watch over the family from beyond the grave, they have always made offerings to dead relatives to ensure that their souls are at peace. In ancient times, even the poorest households kept a shrine like the one in our picture. At New Year, the Chinese family still gathers round and bows deeply in a *kowtow*, to show respect for the ancestors. Since people believed that emperors were like fathers to their subjects, sacrifices to the royal ancestors were especially important. They affected both the emperor's family and the whole country.

Confucius taught that children must be devoted to their parents. Widows were supposed to be eternally chaste, never remarrying. The Chinese family in our photograph still expect the father to be head of the household.

THE FIRST EMPIRE 221 BC–AD 618

Although China was often divided after the first unification in 221 BC, the ideal of one nation ruled by an emperor who was "son of heaven" was never forgotten. The harsh policies of Qin did not last long. Soon the Han took power and ruled with one short interruption for almost 400 years. Envoys were sent to the barbarian kingdoms in the west and pacified the border areas. Philosophers and politicians set up a system of government which lasted for centuries. Taxes were imposed on the whole country and goods were sent from the rich lands of the south to the court, which moved east from Changan to Luoyang in 25 AD.

When the Han collapsed, 300 years of division and civil war followed. The second emperor of the dynasty which reunited the country, the Sui, was Yangdi. He left a permanent legacy to future governments in the shape of a waterway linking the Yangtze delta to the north – the Grand Canal.

Believing that the dead required protection as much as the living, the first emperor of China, Qin Shihuang, made elaborate preparations for building his own tomb. His actual burial chamber has not yet been uncovered, but several enormous pits containing life-size terracotta warriors have been excavated by archaeologists. The warriors were lined up to defend the emperor from hostile forces. Our picture shows one of several enormous antechambers with thousands of warriors and horses. A huge pottery produced the tomb figures, no two of which are identical.

DATECHART

221-211 BC Qin rules China, unifying weights and measures and building roads.

214 BC Sections of defensive walls in north and north-west China are joined to form the Great Wall. It acts as a protection against invaders known as Huns (Chinese *Xiongnu*).

210 BC After the death of the first emperor of Qin, uprisings spread throughout the country.

202 BC The Han, a new ruling house, is founded, proclaiming a return to the ways of the earliest kings.

138-115 BC Zhang Qian, a Han minister, makes two journeys to the far west as part of a determined attempt to quell the *Xiongnu* invaders.

c120-90 BC Sima Qian writes the first official history, the *Records of the Historian*.

AD 25 The later or western Han regime is founded after a period of civil war.

AD 105 Paper is invented by Cai Lun.

AD 220 Cao Cao, a powerful general, defeats the Han and China splits into three kingdoms.

cAD 375-406 Gu Kaizhu lived, China's earliest known great painter.

AD 420-581 The country is divided into rival kingdoms in the north and south.

AD 581 After over 300 years, China is reunified.

AD 605-610 The Grand Canal is built.

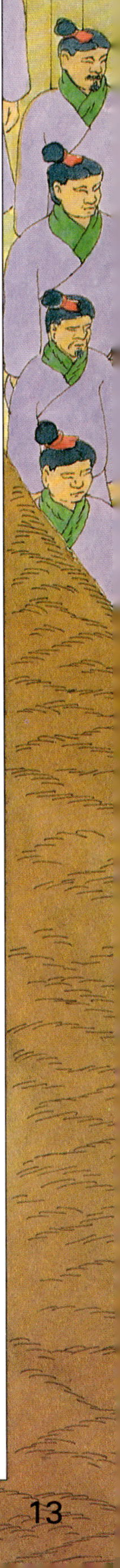

THE FIRST EMPIRE

Qin Shihuang
The first unifier of China (Qin Shihuang means "first emperor of the Qin") was a ruthless leader who was both cruel and talented. He believed that the emperor should rule by force, and punished anyone who displeased him. At the same time, his tough government made useful changes, like standardizing the writing system. He is condemned in China for the episode in our picture. He buried scholars alive and burned ancient books. He was particularly scornful of Confucians, thinking them weak and unrealistic. He favoured a philosophy called "Legalism", which rewarded and punished different kinds of behaviour.

The Great Wall
Qin Shihuang also left a legacy of achievement. He joined up fortifications in the north to make the Great Wall. The Wall was designed to protect China from the raids of the *Xiongnu*. Our picture shows labourers at work beating the earth to make the wall's base.

221 BC–AD 618

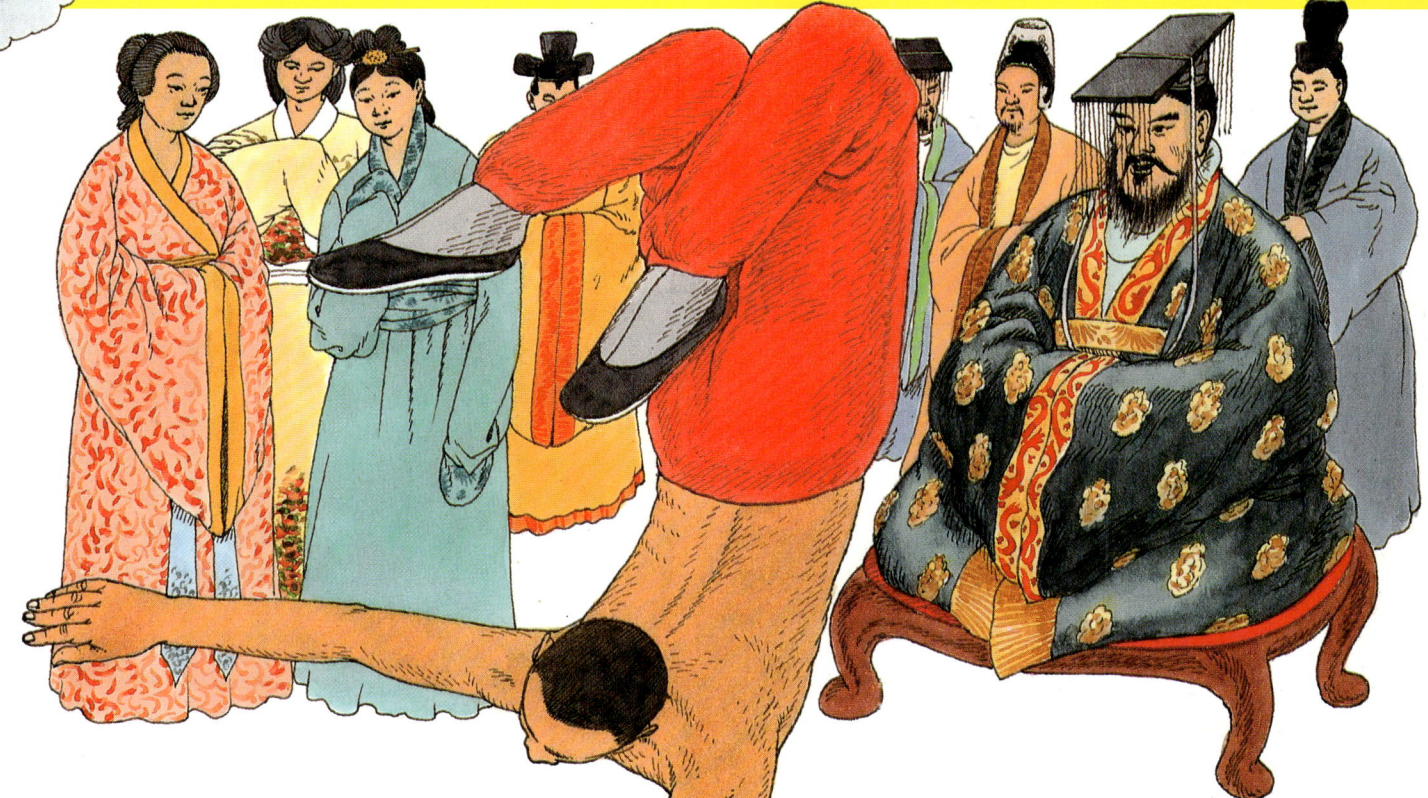

Life at court
The emperor ruled with the assistance of ministers and officials. He had absolute power, and was surrounded by feuding factions hoping to increase their wealth and influence; intrigue at court was a recurring problem. But nobles and courtiers enjoyed a brilliant and lively way of life. Jugglers and acrobats like the one in our picture performed at sumptuous banquets. They were accompanied by musicians playing flutes and drums. From models found in tombs, we know that singers and dancers often performed at feasts for the rich. Upper-class families owned large estates and loved hunting and falconry. They wore fine robes of embroidered silks and women had jewelry of gold and precious stones.

The jade prince
The suit in our picture is made of jade, a beautiful green stone which the Chinese believed acted as a preservative. It was made for the burial of a Han prince and shows how the luxury which aristocrats enjoyed in life went with them to the grave.

THE FIRST EMPIRE

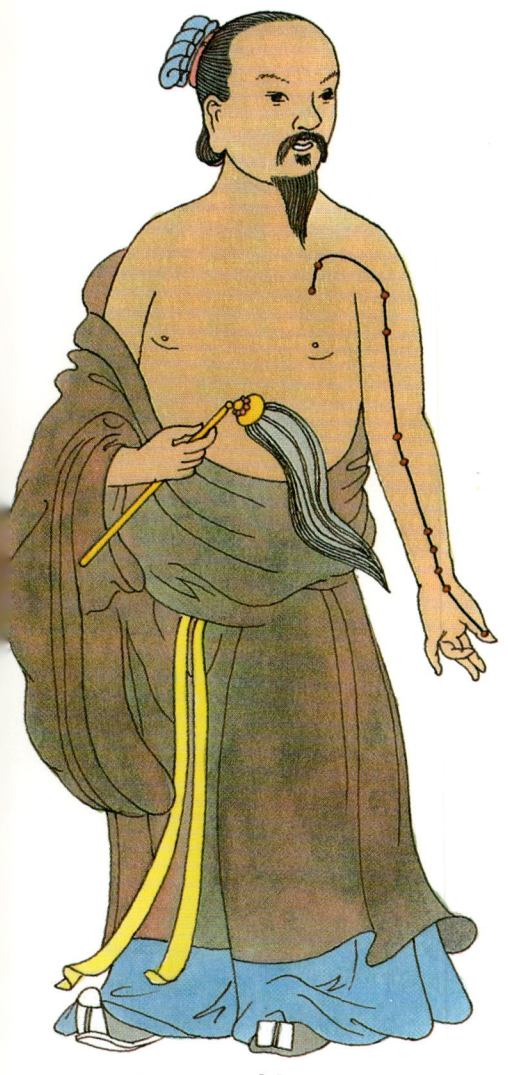

Medicine
Texts from 2,000 years ago show that Chinese doctors had found paths in the body which responded to stimulation by needles. Acupuncture, the science of healing by applying needles, has been used by the Chinese ever since. The picture shows an acupuncture path in the arm. Chinese doctors thought illness could result from too much fire or sluggishness in the body. Heat and cold were part of the patterns of *yang* (male) and *yin* (female), the basic forces running through the universe.

Science and technology
China is the home of many important scientific advances. Enormous engineering feats like the Great Wall and the Grand Canal (shown in the photograph being used today) are well known. But the inventive Chinese also used magnetic compasses and wheelbarrows as early as the Han dynasty. The abacus, a kind of early calculator, was in use in the second century. Astronomers noted comets and eclipses, and engineers built roads and bridges, spurred on by the court's need for efficient communications with all corners of the empire. The illustration shows an impressive system of salt-mining used in the south-west.

Papermaking
Ancient tradition says that Cai Lun invented paper in the first century. Before then, wood and silk were used for writing on. Papermaking, a complicated process illustrated in these scenes from a technical manual, later spread to the west. Printing from wooden blocks is also a Chinese invention. It allowed books to reach large numbers of people because printing is cheaper than writing by hand. The earliest printed book in the world was produced in China.

Cutting and soaking bamboo

Cooking the mixture

221 BC–AD 618

Dipping mould into pulp

Pressing wet paper

Drying on hot wall

17

THE GOLDEN AGE AD 618-1368

The Tang and Song periods saw Chinese culture assuming many of the features it was to retain for the rest of the imperial era. Officials were selected through stiff competitive examinations on Confucian texts. Literary forms – poems, ballads and essays – became fixed. Painters produced fine scrolls. Most of the population lived on the land, but cities also grew up with lively pleasure quarters. There were often rebellions, especially when court life became so lavish that high taxes were needed to support it! This was also the age when courtiers and commoners were devout followers of the Buddhist religion, and when monasteries and temples amassed great wealth. Civil wars broke out in the 10th and 13th centuries. The court had to abandon north China when Mongol power grew in China and throughout the world.

Wen Tianxiang
Many Chinese were devastated when the Song court moved south. A courageous soldier, Wen Tianxiang, fought against the Mongols. But the Song were no match for the Mongol horsemen. Wen was captured, imprisoned and executed. Here he refuses to bow to the Mongols.

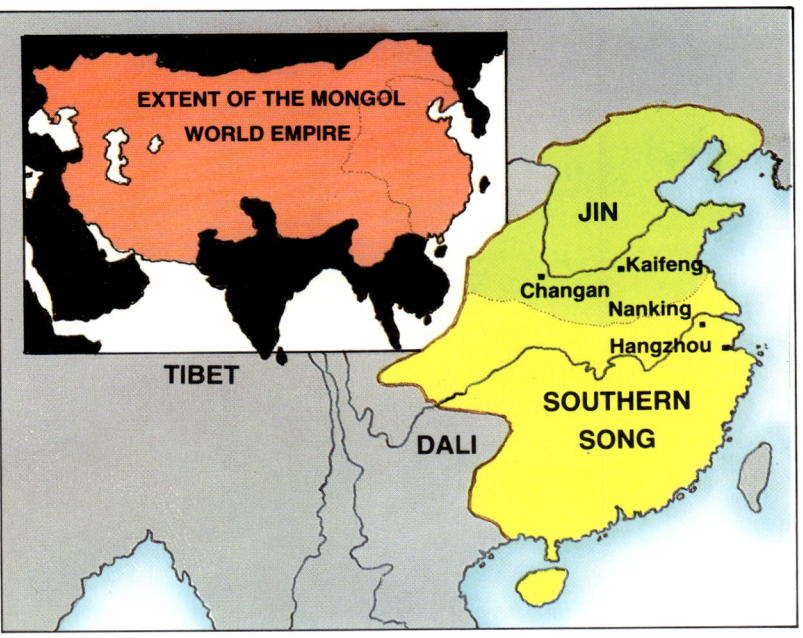

DATECHART

618 The second emperor of the Sui, Yangdi, is assassinated and a new dynasty, the Tang, is founded.

621 A system of competitive civil service examinations is founded. It lasted, with modifications, until the end of imperial times.

755 After a period when culture and the economy flourished to an unprecedented degree, the Tang regime is rocked by the rebellion of An Lushan.

907-960 The Tang finally collapses. A period of civil war follows.

960 Zhao Kuangyin founds the Song dynasty, with its capital at Kaifeng on the Yellow River.

1138 A long period of trouble on the northern borders leads to the capture of north China by the Jurched, a nation of horse-riding warriors. The Song court is forced to flee south to Hangzhou.

1279 After years of war, remnant Song forces surrender to the Mongols under Kubilai Khan, who founds the Yuan dynasty. Gradually the Mongols fall under Chinese influence, and adopt Chinese ways of life.

1275-1292 Marco Polo visits China in the service of Kubilai Khan. His account of the fabulous riches of Cathay enthralled Europeans.

1368 The peasant rebel Zhu Yuanzhang founds the Ming dynasty and drives the Mongols out of China. He establishes the new dynastic capital at Nanking.

THE GOLDEN AGE

Town life

In Tang and especially Song times, cities had grown to an enormous size. Musicians and singers entertained crowds at market places. Pedlars called out their wares, and visitors from all over the country bought fine foods, fabrics and pots at busy market stalls. The city of Changan was the capital of the Tang court. It had a million people and was built on a grid plan on a north-south axis. The palace, facing south, was seen as the symbolic and actual centre of the Chinese empire and of the world itself. The luxurious life of the court went on alongside the humble existence of innkeepers, carters and tradesmen. Craftsmen like silk weavers and silversmiths produced goods for the wealthy consumers of the time. Rich men amused themselves with wine and dancing girls.

AD 618-1368

Theatre

Entertainment flourished in the towns. Markets attracted ballad singers and story tellers. At inns and taverns, working men and soldiers gathered to relax. Opera troupes, like the one in the illustration, would travel from city to city. Performances were brilliant spectacles, with gorgeous costumes and loud music. In Yuan times, rules for opera dress, movement and make-up were formal. The actor in the photograph is applying make-up in the traditional way, using bright colours which help the audience to identify her character.

The life of women

In classical China, women lived to serve and obey their husbands. Women had to cook and look after children, and were not expected to learn to read and write. Court ladies were restricted to their quarters. Many rich men had more than one wife. It was common from Song times onwards for women to bind their feet small, making walking painful. This cruel practice persisted until the early 20th century.

Justice

Ordinary citizens were terrified of the power of government officials. Many stories and operas describe how a suspect could be cruelly punished at the command of a magistrate. Our picture shows prisoners locked into a "cangue" (the Chinese equivalent of the stocks in Europe).

THE GOLDEN AGE

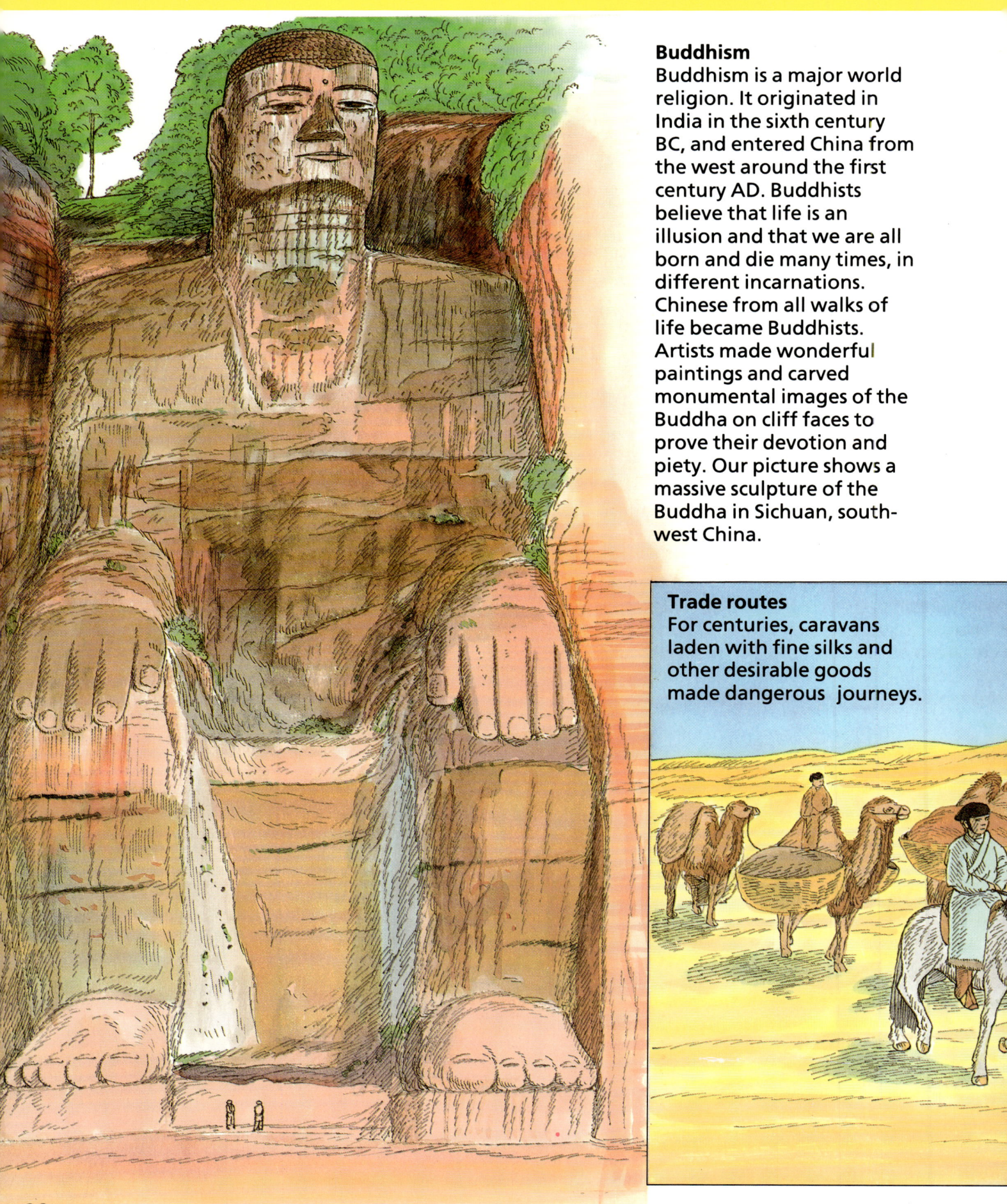

Buddhism
Buddhism is a major world religion. It originated in India in the sixth century BC, and entered China from the west around the first century AD. Buddhists believe that life is an illusion and that we are all born and die many times, in different incarnations. Chinese from all walks of life became Buddhists. Artists made wonderful paintings and carved monumental images of the Buddha on cliff faces to prove their devotion and piety. Our picture shows a massive sculpture of the Buddha in Sichuan, south-west China.

Trade routes
For centuries, caravans laden with fine silks and other desirable goods made dangerous journeys.

AD 618-1368

Poetry

Our picture shows the Song emperor Huizong, who reigned 1101-1126, and the photograph is of one of his paintings. Like most Chinese aristocrats, the emperor composed poetry and practised calligraphy. The Tang and Song periods produced some of China's most famous writers. Their poems describe the beauty of nature and the hardships endured by the common people, contrasted with the corruption and greed of some officials. These poems are still read and loved by Chinese people today.

They travelled overland from metropolitan China through central Asia to the middle east. The caravans took camels to survive the arid conditions on the way. Ideas and cultural influences were exchanged along the trade routes. Marco Polo travelled overland to China from Italy in the 13th century in the service of the Mongols.

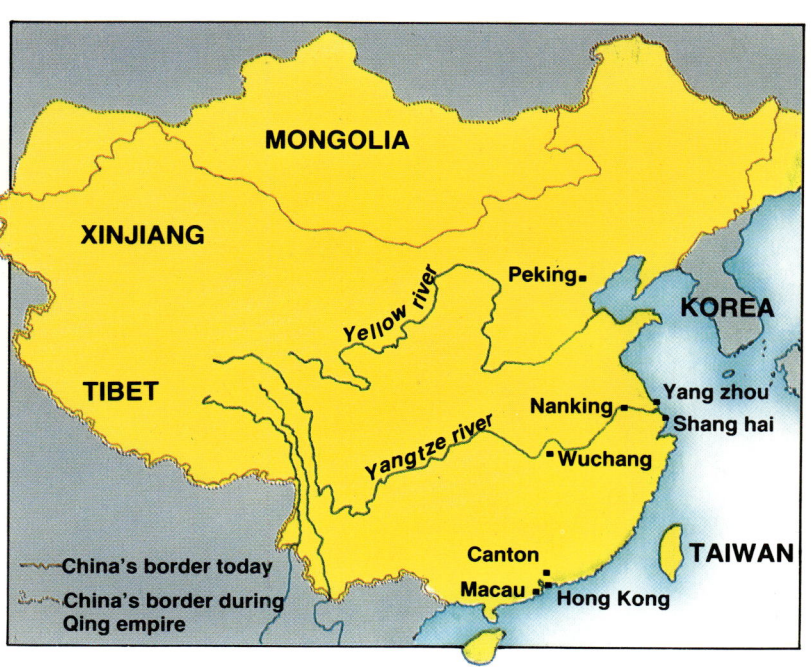

DATECHART

1368-1398 After chasing the Mongols from China, the founder of the Ming dynasty, Zhu Yuanzhang, consolidates his control over the entire country.

1405 The great navigator Zheng He leads voyages of exploration.

1408 The Yongle emperor sponsors the great *Yongle dadian*, a dictionary in 11,000 volumes.

1421 The capital is moved from Nanking to Peking and the court takes up residence in the Forbidden City.

1644 After growing in strength for decades, Manchu forces from the north-east take Peking and found the Qing dynasty. Nurhaci, their leader, becomes the first emperor of the Qing.

1715-1801 Cao Xueqin, author of China's best-loved novel *Dream of the Red Chamber*, lives in an impoverished aristocratic family.

1755-59 The Qing empire's borders expand westward. China absorbs Xinjiang province.

1839-1842 China is humiliated by the western powers in the Opium Wars. Many coastal cities later come under foreign control.

1850-73 Taiping rebellion: south China undergoes upheaval and carnage as rebels try to defeat the Manchus.

1900 Anti-foreign sentiment erupts in north China.

1911 Fall of the Manchu dynasty; founding of the Republic of China.

IMPERIAL SPLENDOUR AD 1368-1911

For over 150 years, China was the eastern flank of the great Mongol world empire. Then the country was reclaimed for the native Han Chinese by a dynasty which took the name Ming, meaning "bright". China entered a period of stability. With its own traditions of medicine, warfare, transportation and the arts, China felt little desire for contact with the outside world.

In 1421 the Yongle emperor moved the court north to Peking, which has been the seat of most Chinese governments ever since. The early 17th century saw the rise of a new power, the Manchus. After defeating the Ming, the Manchus abandoned their nomadic lifestyle and became absorbed into Chinese traditions. Their Qing dynasty ruled China well for 200 years. When western powers demanded to expand trade in the 19th century, the Qing could not resist.

The imperial palace in Peking is known as the Forbidden City because commoners were not allowed to enter. It was first built in the 15th century. In the picture, the emperor walks past his courtiers.

IMPERIAL SPLENDOUR

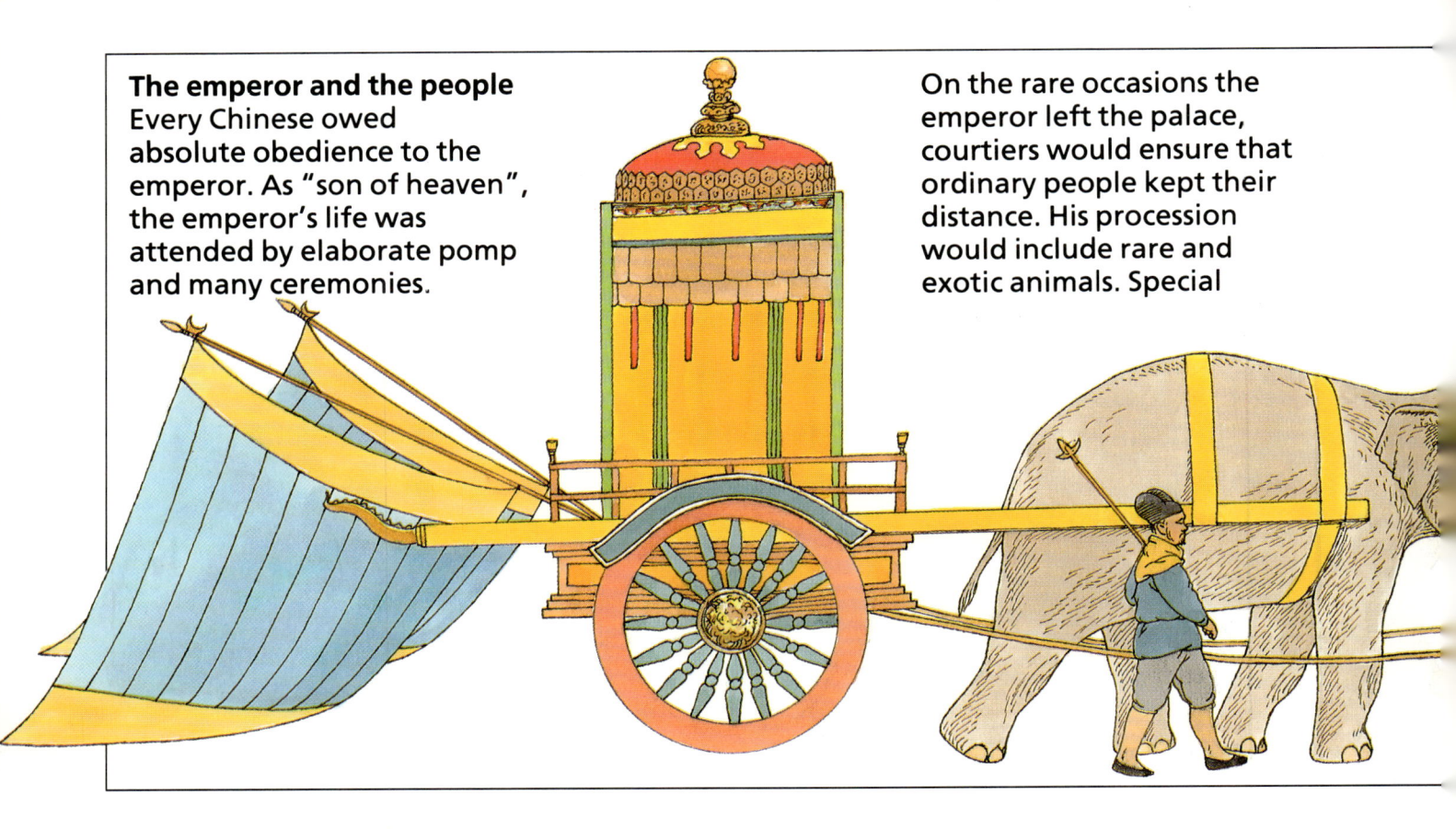

The emperor and the people
Every Chinese owed absolute obedience to the emperor. As "son of heaven", the emperor's life was attended by elaborate pomp and many ceremonies.

On the rare occasions the emperor left the palace, courtiers would ensure that ordinary people kept their distance. His procession would include rare and exotic animals. Special

Agriculture
To feed his family and pay the high taxes which supported court life, the Chinese farmer grew grain. Our picture shows how rice (which is the staple crop of south China) was planted in paddy fields. Methods of growing rice have changed relatively little.

AD 1368-1911

palaces were built for him, even in places he might only visit briefly. The ordinary people thought the emperor was a kind of god, and the magnificence of his train reflected his power. He alone could select officials. He ruled by a system of "memorials". These were reports sent by the magistrates and governors who looked after day-to-day government.

The photograph shows modern Chinese farmers planting rice in south China. In north China, where the weather is colder and drier, wheat has traditionally been grown. Northern Chinese people still like eating noodles and bread, whereas southern Chinese would rather eat rice.

Porcelain
Craftsmen in different parts of the country made bowls and pots of various colours and styles. Chinese porcelain became so famous around the world that today we often call our crockery "china". Our picture shows an artist painting a pot. The artists who decorated porcelain continually experimented with new colours and firing techniques.

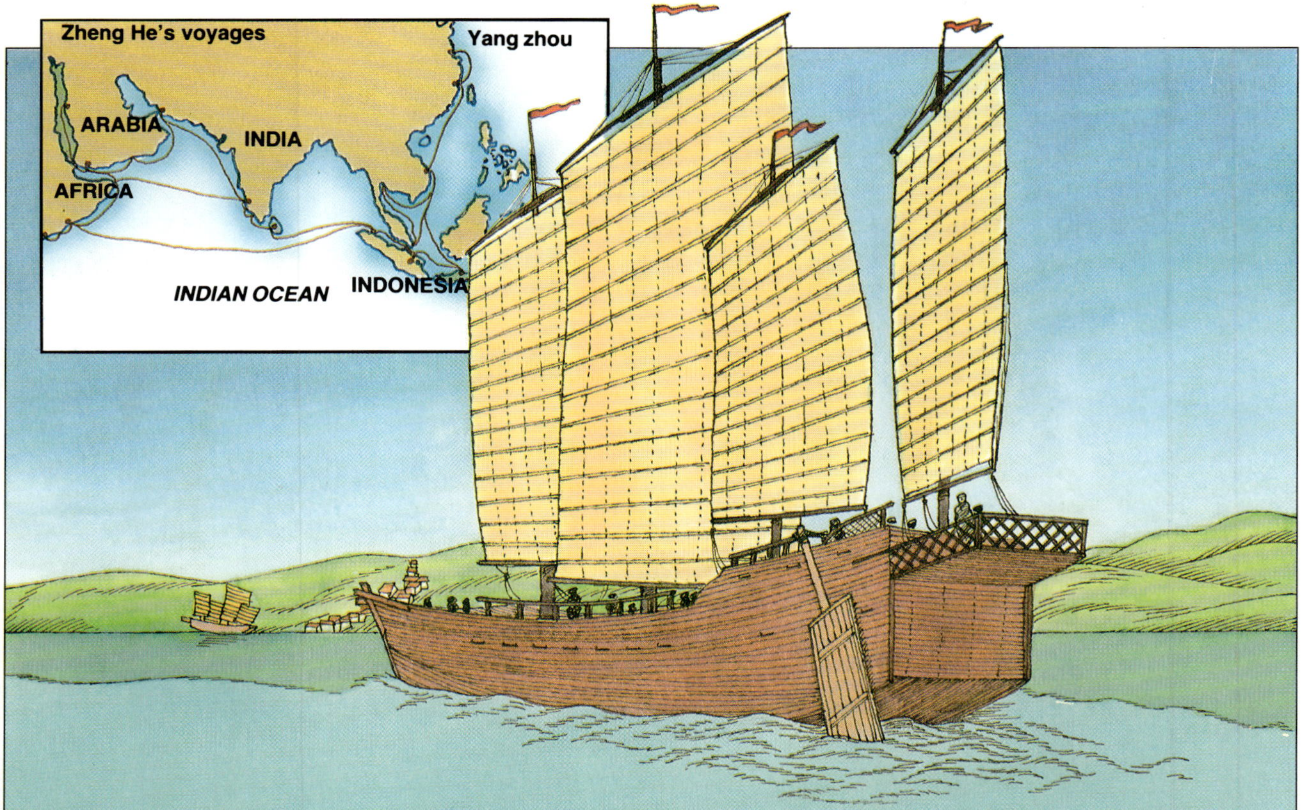

IMPERIAL SPLENDOUR

Exploration
Setting out from southeast China in an enormous wooden ship, Zheng He led a flotilla on seven expeditions. He journeyed through southeast Asia, India and Ceylon to the Gulf of Persia and the east coast of Africa. These journeys of exploration brought back treasure (and also unusual animals like giraffes for the emperor's menagerie) as tribute to the Chinese ruler from distant countries. Zheng He used a maritime compass perfected by Chinese scientists to guide him. His journeys taught the Chinese about distant lands.

Jesuits
China's civilization and culture have long intrigued people in other lands. In the 16th century Jesuit Catholic priests, like the one in our illustration, made the dangerous journey across the world from Europe to China. They hoped to convert the people and rulers of China to Christianity. Their knowledge of astronomy and mathematics impressed Chinese scholars, but few Chinese were persuaded to become Christians.

AD 1368-1911

Opium
In the 19th century, the habit of opium smoking became widespread. Traders sold Chinese teas, silks and ceramics to the west in exchange for opium. Lin Zexu, the political leader in our picture, became so enraged at the harm opium did to the Chinese people that he publicly burned a huge consignment of the drug. The European powers reacted to this act of defiance by sending gunships to China to fight what became known as the "Opium Wars".

The Boxer Rebellion
Several massive social upheavals shook China in the closing years of the Qing dynasty. The government had lost control of large parts of the country. Our picture shows an episode in the war of 1900, when patriotic Chinese soldiers known as "Boxers" attacked British, French, Russian and Japanese forces in China. The Boxers had no modern weapons and were soon defeated. Like many Chinese of the time, they could not understand how their once strong country could be invaded by foreign armies. Soon after the defeat of the Boxers, the Qing dynasty fell, and with it ended a tradition of imperial rule stretching back 2,000 years.

"LET THE PAST SERVE THE PRESENT"

In the early 20th century, China changed from an empire ruled by a god-king to a socialist state governed by political leaders. It was a turbulent period in which civil war and invasion by the Japanese caused millions of deaths. Between 1911 and 1949 the country was split up, with foreign rule in many cities and warlords controlling vast areas. Famines and epidemics occurred regularly. Gradually, a group of revolutionaries under Mao Zedong (later the leader of the People's Republic of China) became the strongest force. Mao's slogan "let the past serve the present" sums up his philosophy: keep the things which make China strong and throw out backward customs which hold up the drive towards modernisation.

China today

China is the world's largest nation, with over a billion people. Most of them still live on the land, but huge cities like Peking and Shanghai are growing. Feeding, clothing and educating the enormous population is the government's biggest headache. Couples are encouraged to have only one child (like the parents on the government poster in the photograph). Over China's enormous area people live and speak in many different ways, but they are united by a common past and by their written language.

Mao Zedong

The man who led China out of the tumultous first half of the 20th century was Mao Zedong. He defeated the Nationalists in 1949 after years of civil war. The Long March, shown in our photograph, was an incredible journey by Mao's army. Mao built China into an independent country. He had bitter memories of China's humiliation by foreign powers, and when he gained power he turned China's back on the outside world. His first priority was to free the peasantry from famine and debt. Since Mao's death in 1976 China has opened up to foreign trade, but many Chinese still admire Mao and his vision of a strong China, proud of her past and confident of her future.

Chinatowns

All over the world, communities of Chinese people are known for their hard-working way of life. Many cities have a Chinatown. The photograph shows the lion dance in London's Chinese area. In Chinese communities all over the world, just as in China itself, thousands of people join in noisy celebrations at Chinese New Year, and watch the lion chase off evil spirits and bring good luck.

Tourism

A few years ago, China was completely isolated from the rest of the world. Now visitors go to China in their millions to see famous sights like the Great Wall and the terracotta warriors. China is repairing old sites and buildings, hoping to attract foreign tourists and the money they bring.

INDEX

A
agriculture, 5, 7, 26, 27
armies, 4, 6, 18, 30
art and crafts, 4, 7, 9, 12, 13, 18, 22, 23, 25, 27
astronomy, 6, 16

B
books, 8, 13, 16, 24
Boxer Rebellion, 29
bronze-casting, 6, 7, 9
Buddhism, 18, 22
burials, 6, 10, 12, 15

C
civil wars, 12, 13, 18, 19, 30
civilization, 4, 6, 28
Confucius, 4, 7, 8, 10, 11
court life, 9, 15, 18, 20, 26

D
dynasties, 5, 6, 7, 12, 13, 14, 16, 18, 19, 20, 23, 24, 25

E
emperors, 4, 5, 11, 12, 13, 14, 15, 19, 23, 24, 26-27
engineering works, 6, 12, 13, 14, 16
entertainment, 15, 20, 21

F
family life, 10, 11
farmers, 4, 5, 26, 27
Forbidden City, 24, 25

G
government, 4, 5, 12, 14, 25, 27
Grand Canal, 12, 13, 16
Great Wall, 13, 14, 16, 31

H
Han dynasty, 12, 13, 16, 25
Huns (*Xiongnu*) 13, 14

I
inventions, 6, 13, 16, 17, 28
iron, 6, 7

J
jewelry, 15
Jurched warriors, 19

K
kings, 5, 8, 13
Kubilai Khan, 19

L
Laozi, 8
Legalism, 14
literature, 4, 18, 21, 23

M
Manchus, 24, 25
Mao Zedong, 30
medicine, 16, 25
Ming dynasty, 5, 19, 24, 25
Mongols, 5, 18, 19, 23, 24, 25

O
Opium Wars, 24, 29

P
papermaking, 13, 16, 17
Peking man, 5
philosophy, 4, 7, 8, 12, 14
poetry, 18, 23
politics, 8, 12
Polo, Marco, 19, 23
pottery, 7, 9, 12, 27

Q
Qin dynasty, 6, 7, 12, 13, 14
Qing dynasty, 24, 25, 29

R
religion, 18, 22
Republic of China, 24, 30

S
science, 6, 13, 16, 28
Shang dynasty, 6, 7, 9
Song dynasty, 18, 19, 20, 21, 23
Sui dynasty, 12, 19

T
Tang dynasty, 18, 19, 20, 23
Taoism, 8
taxes, 4, 12, 18, 26
tombs, 6, 10, 12, 15
town life, 20, 21
trade, 22, 23, 25, 29, 30

W
"Warring States", 6, 7, 8
women, 10, 11, 21
writing, 6, 7, 9, 14, 16, 23

Y
Yuan dynasty, 19, 21

Z
Zhou dynasty, 6, 7

Photographic Credits:
Pages 9, 15, 26 and 31: Robert Harding; pages 11 and 20: Richard and Sally Greenhill; pages 17 and 30-31: Hutchison Library; page 30: Anglo-Chinese Society.